Made in United States
Orlando, FL
01 March 2025

59056639R00056